LEWIS CARROLL

Wonderland

PADMORE PUBLISHING GROUP

LEWIS CARROLL IN WONDERLAND

A BOY'S JOURNEY TO WONDERLAND

Cover design: Julia Arenas

© Cover: Padmore Publishing Group

LEWIS CARROLL
IN
WONDERLAND

BY

Belle Moses

> how a shy boy found his voice
> and became one of the most
> famous writers in the world

Introduction

Lewis Carroll discovered a new country, simply by rowing up and down a river, and telling a story to the accompaniment of dipping oars and rippling waters, as the boat glided through. It is not everyone who can discover a country, people in it with marvelous, fanciful shapes, and give it a place in our mental geography. But Lewis Carroll was not "everyone"—in fact he was like no one else to the many who called him friend. He had the magic power of creating something out of nothing, and gave to the eager children something to think about, to guess about, and to talk about.

If he had written nothing else but "Alice in Wonderland," that one book would have been quite enough to make him famous, but his pen was never idle, and the world of children has much for which to thank him.

In telling the story of his childhood up to he became a man, I am indebted to many, for courtesy and assistance. I wish specially to thank my brother, Montrose J. Moses. Columbia Library, Astor Library, St. Agnes Branch of the Public Library, and Miss Brown, of the Traveling Library, who have all been exceedingly kind and helpful. To E. P. Dutton and Company I extend my thanks for permission to quote from Miss Isa Bowman's interesting reminiscences, and to the American and English editors of *The Strand* I am also indebted for a similar courtesy.

Belle Moses
New York

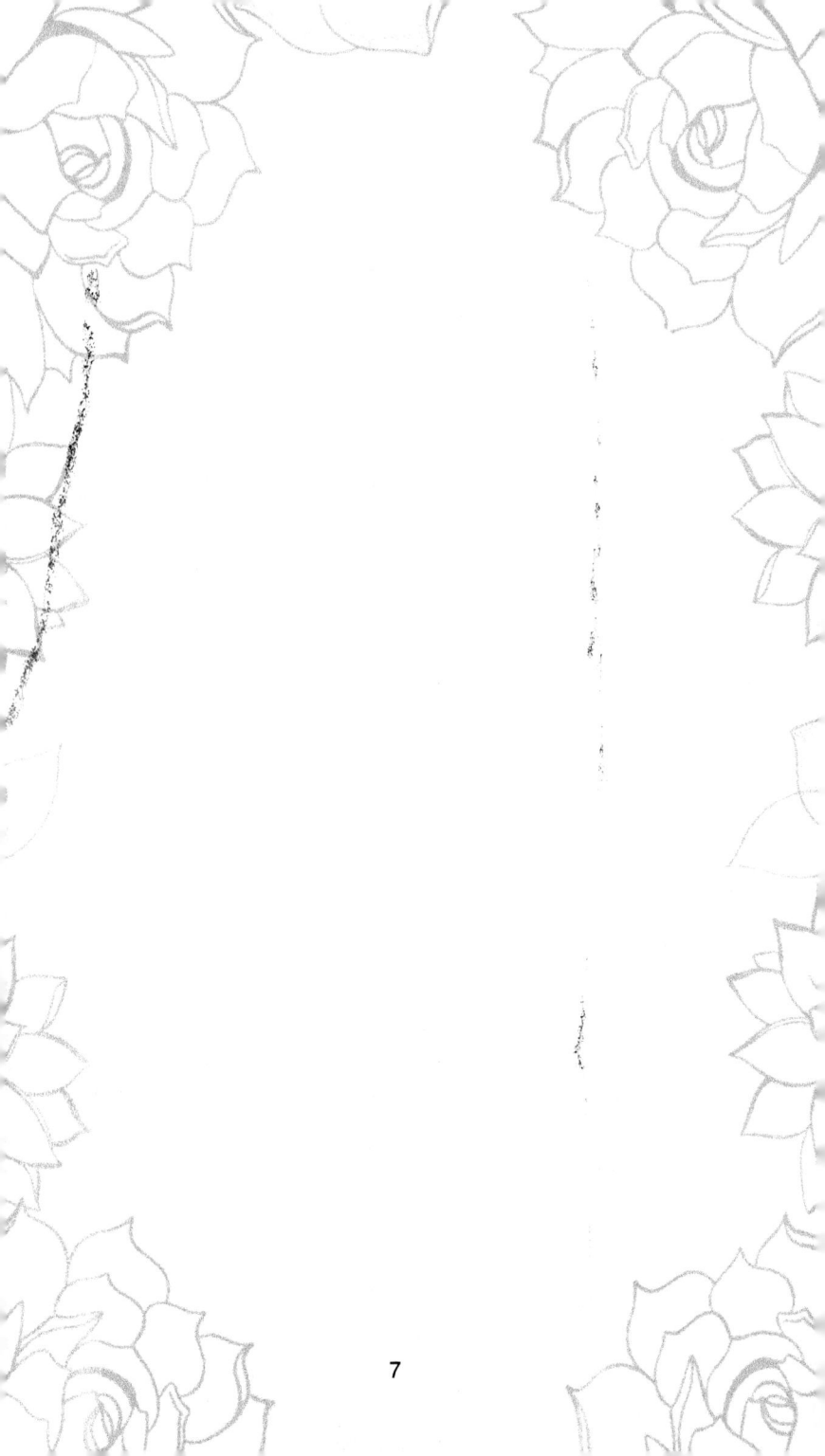

FAMILY TREE

ELIZABETH COULTON (????- 1744)

REVEREND CRISTOPHER DODGSON (1686?-20 June 1750)

MARY FRANCES SMYTH (1749-1796)

CHARLES DODGSON MA (1721 - 1795)

THOMAS DOGDSON (1775-1794)

PERCY CURRER DOGDSON (1782-1807)

CAPT. CHARLES DODGSON (1769 - 1803)

ELIZABETH ANNE DOGDSON (1770 - 1836)

LUCY HUME (1775-1818)

CHARLES LUTWIDGE (1768-1848)

They were first cousins

CHARLES DODGSON MA (1800-1868)

FRANCES JANE LUTWIDGE (1803-1851)

CHARLES LUTWIDGE DODGSON (LEWIS CARROLL) 1832-1898

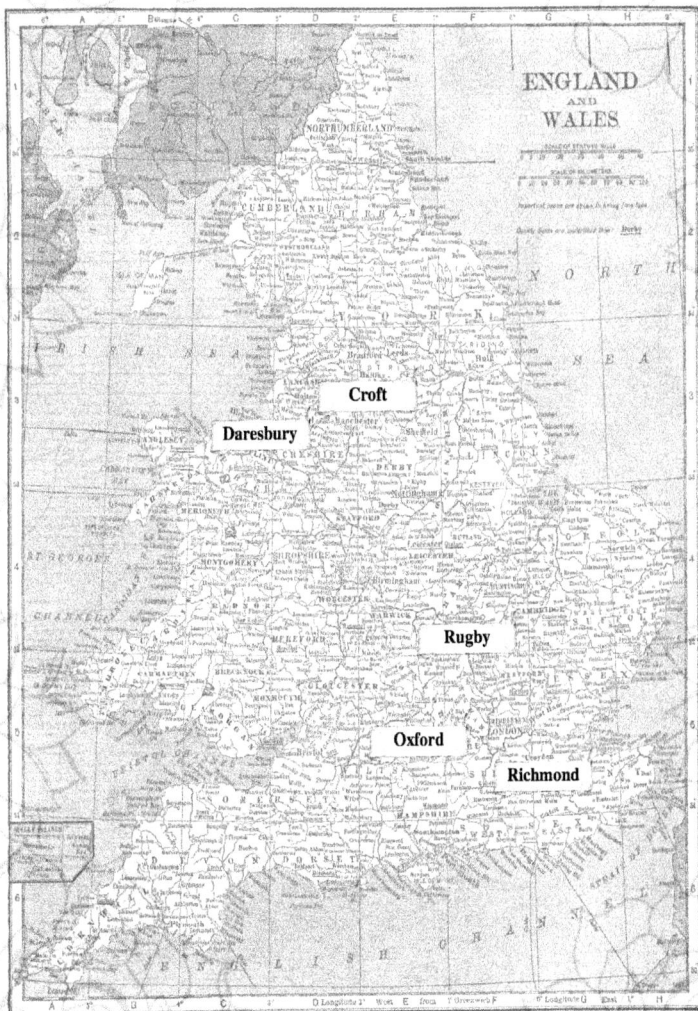

PLACES HE LIVED

ENGLAND
AND
WALES

Croft

Daresbury

Rugby

Oxford

Richmond

chapter I.

THERE
WAS
ONCE A
LITTLE
BOY.

here was once a little boy whose name was *not* Lewis Carroll. He was christened Charles Lutwidge Dodgson, in the parish church of Daresbury, England, where he was born, on January 27, 1832. A little out-of-the-way village was Daresbury, a name derived from a word meaning oak, and Daresbury was certainly famous for its beautiful oaks.

The christening of Baby Charles must have been a very happy occasion. To begin with, the tiny boy was the first child of what proved to be a "numerous family," and the officiating clergyman was the proud papa. The name of Charles had been bestowed upon the eldest son for generations of Dodgsons, who had carried it honorably through the line, handing it down untarnished to this latest Charles, in the parish church at Daresbury.

The Dodgsons could doubtless trace their descent much further back than a great-great-grandfather, being a race of gentlemen and scholars, but the Rev. Christopher Dodgson, who lived quite a century before Baby Charles saw the light, is the earliest ancestor we hear of, and he held a living in Yorkshire.

In those days, a clergyman was dependent upon some noble patron for his living, a living meaning the parish of which he had charge and the salary he received for his work, and so when the Rev. Christopher's eldest son Charles also took holy orders, he had for *his* patron the Duke of Northumberland, who gave him the living of Elsden in Northumberland, a cold, bleak, barren country.

The Rev. Charles took what fell to his lot with much philosophy and a saving sense of humor. He suffered terribly from the cold despite the fact that he snuggled down between two feather beds in the big parlor, which was no doubt the best room in a most uncomfortable house. It was all he could do to keep from freezing, for the doors were rarely closed against the winds that howled around them. The good clergyman was firmly convinced that the end of the world would come by frost instead of fire. Even when safely in bed, he never felt *quite* comfortable unless his head was wrapped in three nightcaps, while he twisted a pair of stockings, like a cravat, around his suffering throat. He generally wore two shirts at a time, as washing was cheap,

and rarely took off his coat and his boots.

This uncomplaining, jovial clergyman finally received his reward. King George III bestowed upon him the See of Elphin, which means that he was made bishop, and had no more hardships to bear. This gentleman, who was the great-grandfather of our Charles, had four children; Elizabeth Anne, the only daughter, married a certain Charles Lutwidge of Holmrook in Cumberland.

They had two sons. Charles, the eldest, entered the army and rose to the rank of captain in the 4th Dragoon Guards. He lost his life in the performance of a perilous duty, leaving behind him two sons; Charles, the elder, turned back into the ways of his ancestors and became a clergyman, and Hassard, who studied law, had a brilliant career.

This last Charles, in 1830, married Frances Jane Lutwidge, and in 1832 we find him baptizing another little Charles, our Charles (later known as Lewis Carroll), in the parish church at Daresbury, his eldest son, and consequently his pride and hope. The living at Daresbury was the beginning of a long life of service to the Church. The father of our Charles rose to be one of the foremost clergymen of his time, a man of wide learning, of deep piety, and of great charity, beloved by rich and poor. Though of somewhat sober nature, in moments of recreation he could throw off his cares like a boy, delighting his friends by his wit and humor, and the rare gift of telling anecdotes, a gift his son inherited in full measure, long before he took the name of "Lewis Carroll," some twenty years after he was received into the fold of the parish church at Daresbury.

Little Charles headed the list of eleven young Dodgsons, and the mother of this infant brigade was a woman in a thousand. We all know what mothers are; then we can imagine this one, so kind and gentle that never a harsh word was known to pass her lips, and may be able to trace her quiet, helpful influence on the character of our Boy, just as we see her delicate features reproduced in many of his later pictures.

A boy must be a poor specimen, indeed, if such a father and mother could not bring out the best in him. Saddled as he was, with the responsibility of being the oldest of eleven, and consequently an example held up to younger brothers and sisters, Charles was grave and serious beyond his years. Only an eldest child can appreciate what a responsibility this really is. You mustn't do "so and so" for fear one of the younger ones might do likewise!

If his parents had not been very remarkable people, this same Charles might have developed into a virtuous little prig. "Good Brother Charles who never does wrong" might have grown into a terrible bugbear to the other small Dodgsons, had he not been brimful of fun and humor himself. As it was he soon became their leader in all their games and plays, and the quiet parsonage on the glebe farm, full a mile and a half from even the small traffic of the village, rang at least with the echoes of laughter and chatter from these youngsters with strong healthy lungs.

We cannot be quite sure whether they were good children or bad children, for time somehow throws a halo around childhood, but let us hope they were just middling. We cannot bear to think of all those prim little saints, with ramrods down their backs, sitting sedately on a Sunday in the family pew — perhaps it took two family pews to hold them — with folded hands and pious expressions. We can't believe these Dodgsons were so silly; they were reverent little souls doubtless, and probably were not bad in church, but oh! let us hope they got into mischief sometimes. There was plenty of room for it in the big farm parsonage.

Glebe farms were very common in England; they consisted of large tracts of land surrounding the parsonage, which the pastor was at liberty to cultivate for his own use, or to increase his often scanty income, and as the parsonage at Daresbury was comparatively small, and the glebe or farm lands fairly large, we can be sure these boys and girls loved to be outdoors, and little Charlie at a very early age began to number some queer companions among his intimate friends.

His small hands burrowing in the soft, damp earth, brought up squirming, wriggling things— earthworms, snails, and the like. He made pets of them, studying their habits in his "small boy" way, and having long, serious talks with them, lying on the ground beside them as they crawled around him.

An anthill was to him a tiny town, and many a long hour the child must have spent busying himself in their small affairs, settling imaginary disputes, helping the workers, supplying provisions in the way of crumbs, and thus early beginning to understand the ways of the woodland things about

which he loved to write years after. He had, for
boon companions, certain toads, with whom he held
animated conversations, and it is said that he really
taught earthworms the art of warfare by supplying
them with small pieces of pipe with which to fight.

He did not, like Hiawatha in the legend, "Learn of
every bird its language," but he invented a language
of his own, in which no doubt he discoursed wisely to
the toads and snails who had time to listen; he learned
to speak this language quite fluently, so that in later
years when eager children clustered about him, and
with wide eyes and peals of laughter listened to his
nonsense verses, full of the queerest words they ever

animals were
his friends

heard, they could still understand from the very tones of his voice exactly what he meant.

Indeed, when little Charles Lutwidge Dodgson grew up to be Lewis Carroll, he worked this funny language of his by equally funny rules, so that, as he said, "a perfectly balanced mind could understand it." Of course, there were other companions for the Dodgson children—cats and dogs, and horses and cows, and in the village of Warrington, seven miles away, there were children to be found of their own size and age, but Daresbury itself was very lonely.

A canal ran through the far end of the parish, and here bargemen used to ply to and fro, carrying produce and fodder to the nearby towns. Mr. Dodgson took a keen interest in these men who seemed to have no settled

coach

place of worship. In a quiet persuasive way he suggested to Sir Francis Egerton, a large landholder of the country, that it would be nice to turn one of the barges into a chapel, describing how it could be done for a hundred pounds, well knowing, clever man, that he was talking to a most interested listener; for a few weeks later he received a letter from Sir Francis telling him that the chapel was ready. In this odd little church, the first of its kind, Mr. Dodgson preached every Sunday evening.

But at Daresbury itself life was very monotonous; even the passing of a cart was a great event, and going away was a great adventure. There was one never-to-be-forgotten occasion when the family went off on a holiday jaunt to Beaumaris. Railroads were then very rare things, so they made the journey in three days by coach, allowing also three days for the return trip.

It was great fun traveling in one of those old-time coaches with all the luggage strapped behind, and all the bright young faces atop, and four fast-trotting horses dashing over the ground, and a nice long holiday with fine summer weather to look forward to. But in winter, in those days, traveling was a serious matter; only a favored few could squeeze into the body of the coach; the others still sat atop, muffled to the chin, yet numb with the cold, as the horses went faster and faster, and the wind whistled by, and one's breath froze on the way. Let us hope the little Dodgsons went in the summer time.

Daresbury must have been a beautiful place, with its pleasant walks, its fine meadows, its deep secluded woods, and best of all, those wonderful oak trees which the boy loved to climb, and under whose shade he would lie by the hour, filling his head with all those quaint fancies which he has since given to the world. He was a clever little fellow, eager to learn, and from the first his father superintended his education, being himself a scholar of very high order. He had the English idea of sending his eldest son along the path he himself had trod; first to a public school, then to Oxford, and finally into the Church, if the boy had any leaning that way.

Education in those days began early, and not by way of the kindergarten; the small boy had scarcely lost his baby lisp before he was put to the study of Latin and Greek, and Charles, besides, developed a passion for mathematics. It is told that when a very small boy he showed his father a book of logarithms, asking him to explain it, but Mr. Dodgson mildly though firmly refused.

"You are too young to understand such a difficult subject," he replied; "a few years later you will enjoy the study—wait a while."

"*But*," persisted the boy, his mind firmly bent on obtaining information, "please explain."

Whether the father complied with his request is not recorded, but we rather believe that explanations were set aside for the time. Certain it is, they were demanded again and again, for the boy soon developed a wonderful head for figures and signs, a knowledge which grew with the years, as we shall see later.

When he was still quite a little boy, his mother and father went to Hull to visit Mrs. Dodgson's father who had been ill. The children, some five or six in number—the entire eleven had not yet arrived— were left in the care of an accommodating aunt, but Charles, being the eldest, received a letter from his mother in which he took much pride, his one idea being to keep it out of the clutches of his little sisters, whose hands were always ready for mischief. He wrote upon the back of the note, forbidding them to touch his property, explaining cunningly that it was covered with slimy pitch, a most uncomfortable warning, but it was "the ounce of prevention," for the letter has been handed down to us, and a sweet, cheery letter it was, so full of mother-love and care, and tender pride in the little brood at home. No wonder he prized it! This is probably the first letter he ever received, and it takes very little imagination to picture the important air with which he carried it about, and the care with which he hoarded it through all the years.

There is a dear little picture of our Boy taken when he was eight years old. Photography was not yet in use, so this black print of him is the copy of a silhouette which was the way people had their "pictures taken" in those days. It was always a profile picture, and little Charles's finely shaped head, with its slightly bulging forehead and delicate features, stands sharply outlined. We have also a silhouette of Mrs. Dodgson, and the resemblance between the two is very marked.

When the boy was eleven, a great change came into his life. Sir Robert Peel, the famous statesman, presented to his father the Crown living of Croft, a Yorkshire village about three miles from Darlington. A Crown living is always an exceptionally good one, as it is usually given by royal favor, and accompanied by a comfortable salary. Mr. Dodgson was sorry to leave his old parishioners and the little parsonage where he had seen so much quiet happiness, but he was glad at the same time to get away from the dullness and monotony of Daresbury. With a growing family of children it was absolutely necessary to come more into contact with people, and Croft was a typical, delightful English town, famous for its baths and medicinal waters. Before Mr. Dodgson's time it was an important posting-station for the coaches running between London and Edinburgh, and boasted of a fine hotel near the rectory, used later by gentlemen in the hunting season.

Mr. Dodgson's parish consisted not only of Croft proper, but included the neighboring hamlets of Halnaby, Dalton and Stapleton, so he was a pretty busy man going from one to the other, and the little Dodgsons were busy too, making new friends and settling down into their new and commodious quarters. The village of Croft is on the river Tees,

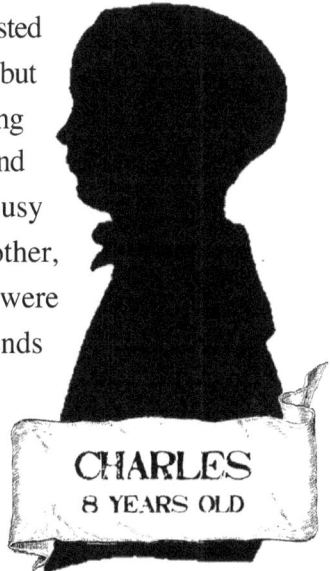

CHARLES
8 YEARS OLD

in fact it stands on the dividing line between Yorkshire and Durham. A bridge divides the two counties, and midway on it is a stone which marks the boundary line. It was an old custom for certain landholders to stand on this bridge at the coming of each new Bishop of Durham, and to present him with an old sword, with an appropriate address of welcome. This sword the Bishop returned immediately.

The Tees often overflowed its banks—indeed, floods were not infrequent in these smiling English landscape countries, kept so fertile and green by the tiny streams which intersect them. Two or three heavy rainfalls will swell the waters, sending them rushing over the country with enormous force. Jean Ingelow in her poem "High Tide on the Coast of Lincolnshire" paints a vivid picture of the havoc such a flood may make in a peaceful land:

> "Where the river, winding down,
> Onward floweth to the town."

But the quaint old church at Croft has doubtless weathered more than one overflow from the restless

river Tees. The rectory, a large brick house, with a sloping tile roof and tall chimneys, stood well back in a very beautiful garden, filled with all sorts of rare plants, intersected by winding gravel paths. As

in all English homes, the kitchen garden was a most attractive spot; its high walls were covered with luxuriant fruit trees, and everybody knows that English "wall fruit" is the most delicious kind. The trees are planted very close to the wall, and the spreading boughs, when they are heavy with the ripening fruit, are not bent with the weight of it, but are thoroughly propped and supported by these walls of solid brick, so the undisturbed fruit comes to a perfect maturity without any of the accidents which occur in the ordinary orchard. The garden itself was bright with kitchen greens, filled with everything needed for household use.

With so much space the little Dodgsons had room to grow and "multiply" to the full eleven, and fine times they had with plays and games, usually invented by their clever brother. One of the principal diversions was a toy railroad with "stations" built at various sections of the garden, usually very pretty and rustic looking, planned and built by Charles

himself. He also made a rude train out of a wheelbarrow, a barrel, and a small truck, and was able to convey his passengers comfortably from station to station, exacting fare at each trip.

He was something of a conjurer, too, and in wig and gown, could amaze his audience for hours with his inexhaustible supply of tricks. He also made some quaint-looking marionettes, and a theater for them to act in, even writing the plays, which were masterpieces in their way. Once he traced a maze upon the snow-covered lawn of the rectory.

Mazes were often found in the real old-time gardens of England; they consisted of intersecting paths bordered by clipped shrubbery and generally arranged in geometrical designs, very puzzling to the unwary person who got lost in them, unable to discover a way out, until by some happy accident the right path was found. "Threading the Maze" was a fashionable pastime in the days of the Tudors; the maze at Hampton Court being one of the most remarkable of that period.

Charles's early knowledge of mathematics made his work on the snow-covered lawn all the more remarkable, for the love of that particular branch of learning certainly grew with his growth. Meanwhile, it was a very serious, earnest little boy, who looked down the long line of Dodgsons, saying with a choke in his voice: "I must leave you and this lovely rectory, and this fair, smiling countryside, and go to school."

He was shy, and the thought struck terror; but everybody who is anybody in England goes to some fine public school before becoming an Oxford or a Cambridge student, and for that reason Charles Lutwidge Dodgson buried his regrets beneath a smiling face, bade farewell to his household, and at the mature age of twelve, armed with enough Greek and Latin to have made a dictionary, with a knowledge of mathematics that a college "don" might well have envied, set forth to this alluring world of books and learning.

chapter II.

SCHOOL DAYS AT RICHMOND AND RUGBY

ith the removal to Croft, Mr. Dodgson, Charles father, was brought more and more into prominence; he was appointed examining chaplain to the Bishop of Ripon, and finally he was made Archdeacon of Richmond and one of the Canons of Ripon Cathedral.

The Grammar School at Richmond was well known in that section of England. It was under the rule of a certain Mr. Tate, whose father, Dr. Tate, had made the school famous some years before, and it was there that our Boy had his first taste of school life. Holidays in those days were not arranged as they are now, for one of the first letters of Charles, sent home from Richmond, was dated August 5th; so it is probable that the term began in midsummer. This special letter was written to his two eldest sisters and gives an excellent picture of those first days, when as a "new boy" he suffered at the hands of his schoolmates.

As advanced as he was in Latin and Greek and mathematics, this letter, for a twelve-year-old boy, does not show any remarkable progress in English. The spelling was precise and correct, but the punctuation was peculiar, to say the least. Still his description of the school life, when one overcame the presence of commas and the absence of periods, presented a vivid picture to the mind.

He tells of the funny tricks the boys played upon him because he was a "new boy." One was called "King of the Cobblers." He was told to sit on the ground while the boys gathered around him and to say "Go to work"; immediately they all fell upon him, and kicked and knocked him about pretty roughly. Another trick was "The Red Lion," and was played in the churchyard; they made a mark on a tombstone and one of the boys ran toward it with his finger pointed and eyes shut, trying to see how near he could get to the mark. When *his* turn came, and he walked toward the tombstone, some boy who stood ready beside it, had his mouth open to bite the outstretched finger on its way to the mark. He closes his letter by stating three uncomfortable things connected with his arrival—the loss of his toothbrush and his failure to clean his teeth for several days in consequence; his inability to find his blotting-paper, and his lack of a shoe-horn.

The games the Richmond boys played—football, wrestling, leapfrog and fighting—he slurred over contemptuously, they held no attraction for him. A schoolboy or girl of the present day can have no ideaof the discomforts of school life in Charles

Dodgson's time, and the boy whose gentle manners were the result of sweet home influence and association with girls, found the rough ways of the English schoolboy a constant trial. Strong and active as he was, he was always up in arms for those weaker and smaller than himself. Bullying enraged him, and distasteful as it was, he soon learned the art of using his fists for the protection of himself and others.

These were the school-days of *Nicholas Nickleby*, *David Copperfield*, and *Little Paul Dombey*. Of course, all schoolmasters were not like *Squeers* or *Creakle*, nor all schoolmasters' wives like *Mrs. Squeers*, nor indeed all schools like Dotheboys' Hall or Salem Hall, or *Dr. Blimber's* cramming establishment, but many of the inconveniences were certainly prominent in the best schools.

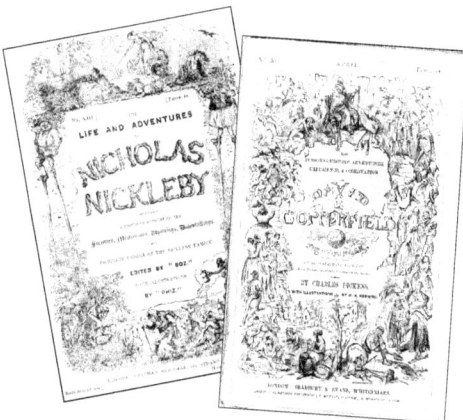

Flogging, or punishment with a stick, was considered the surest road to knowledge; kind, honest, liberal-minded teachers kept a birch-rod and a ferrule within gripping distance, and the average schoolboy thus treated like a little beast, could be pardoned for behaving like one.

In spring or summer the big, bare, comfortless schoolhouses were all very well, but when the days grew chill, the small boy shivered on his hard bench in his draughty corner, and in winter time the scarcity of fires was trying to ordinary flesh and blood. The poor unfortunate who rose at six, and had to fetch and carry his own water from an outdoor pump, or if he had taken the precaution to draw it the night before, had found it frozen in his pitcher, was not to be blamed if washing was merely a figure of speech.

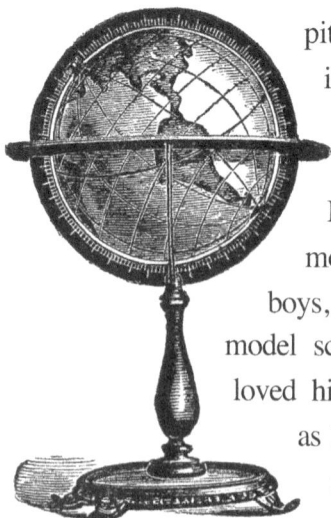

Mr. and Mrs. Tate were most considerate to their boys, and Richmond was a model school of its class. Charles loved his "kind old schoolmaster" as he called him, and he was not alone in this feeling, for

Mr. Tate's influence over the boys was maintained through the affection and respect they had for him. Of course he let them "fight it out" among themselves according to the boy-nature; but the earnest little fellow with the grave face and the eager, questioning eyes, attracted him greatly, and he began to study him in his keen, kind way, finding much to admire and praise in the letters which he wrote to his father, and predicting for him a bright career. Admitting that he had found young Dodgson superior to other boys, he wisely suggested that he should never know this fact, but should learn to love excellence for its own sake, and not for the sake of excelling.

Charles made quite a name for himself during those first school days. Mathematics still fascinated him and Latin grew to be second nature; he stood finely in both, and while at Richmond, he developed another taste: the love of composition, often contributing to the school magazine.

One special story recorded was called "The Unknown One," but doubtless many a rhyme and jingle which could be traced to him found its way into this same little magazine, not forgetting odd sketches which he began to do at a very early age. They were all rough, for the most part grotesque, but full of simple fun and humor, for the quiet studious schoolboy loved a joke.

Charles stayed at the Richmond school for three years; then he took the next step in an English boy's life, he entered Rugby, one of the great public schools. In America, a public school is a school for the people, where free instruction is given to all alike; but the English public school is another thing. It is a school for gentlemen's sons, where tuition fees are far from small, and "extras" mount up on the yearly bills.

Rugby had become a very celebrated school when the great Dr. Arnold was Headmaster. Up to that time it was neither so well known nor so popular as Eton, but Dr. Arnold had governed it so vigorously that his hand was felt long after his untimely death, which occurred just four years before Charles was ready to enter the school. The Headmaster at that time was, strangely enough, named Tait, spelt a little differently from the Richmond schoolmaster. Dr. Tait, who afterwards became Archbishop of Canterbury, was a most capable man, who governed the school for two of the three years that our Boy was a pupil. The last year, Dr. Goulburn was Headmaster.

RUGBY SCHOOL MAP OF BOUNDS

SMALL BACK STREETS IN TOWN ARE OUT OF BOUNDS. OUTSIDE OPEN COUNTRY IS IN BOUNDS

HEAD MASTERS HOUSE

TOWN OF RUGBY

STREETS OUT OF BOUNDS ARE SPOTTED

ENLARGED GROUND PLAN OF RUGBY SCHOOL

(NEW BUILDINGS ARE SPOTTED)

MAP OF RUGBY FIELD

THOMAS ARNOLD, D.D.

MASTER OF RUGBY SCHOOL IN TOM BROWN'S TIME

Charles found Rugby a great change from the quiet of Richmond. He went up in February of 1846, the beginning of the second term, when football was in full swing. The teams practiced on the broad open campus known as "Big-side," and a "new boy" could only look on and applaud the great creatures who led the game.

Rugby was swarming with boys—three hundred at least —from small fourteen-year-olders of the lowest "form," or class, to those of eighteen or twenty of the fifth and sixth, the highest forms. They treated little Dodgson in their big, burly, schoolboy fashion, hazed him to their hearts' content when he first entered, shrugging their shoulders good-naturedly over his love of study, in preference to the great games of cricket and football.

To have a fair glimpse of our Boy's life at this period, some little idea of Rugby and its surroundings might serve as a guide. Those who visit the school today, with its pile of modern, convenient, and ugly architecture, have no conception of what it was then and even in 1846 it bore no resemblance to the original school founded by one Lawrence Sheriffe, "citizen and grocer of London" during the reign of Henry VIII. To begin with, it is situated in Shakespeare's own country,

Warwickshire on the Avon River, and that in itself was enough to rouse the interest of any musing, bookish boy like Charles Dodgson.

From "Tom Brown's School Days," that ever popular book by Thomas Hughes, we may perhaps understand the feelings of the "new boy" just passing through the big, imposing school gates, with the oriel window above, and entering historic Rugby. What first struck his view was the great school field or "close" as they called it, with its famous elms, and next, "the long line of gray buildings, beginning with the chapel and ending with the schoolhouse, the residence of the Headmaster where the great flag was lazily waving from the highest round tower."

As we follow *Tom Brown* through *his* first day, we can imagine our Boy's sensations when he found himself in this howling wilderness of boys. The eye of a boy is as keen as that of a girl regarding dress, and before *Tom Brown*

tom brown's
school days

was allowed to enter Rugby gates he was taken into the town and provided with a cat-skin cap, at seven and sixpence.

"'You see,' said his friend as they strolled up toward the school gates, in explanation of his conduct, 'a great deal depends on how a fellow cuts up at first. If he's got nothing odd about him and answers straightforward, and holds his head up, he gets on.'"

Having passed the gates, *Tom* was taken first to the matron's room, to deliver up his trunk key, then on a tour of inspection through the schoolhouse hall which opened into the quadrangle. This was "a great room, thirty feet long and eighteen high or thereabouts, with two great tables running the whole length, and two large fireplaces at the side with blazing fires in them." This hall led into long dark passages with a fire at the end of each, and this was the hallway upon which the studies opened.

Now, to Charles Dodgson as well as to *Tom Brown*, a study, as they called their rooms, conjured up untold luxury; it was in truth a "Rugby boy's citadel" usually six feet long and four feet broad. It was rather a gloomy light which came in through the bars and grating of the one window, but these precautions had to be taken with the studies on the ground floor, to keep the small boys from slipping out after "lock-up" time.

Under the window was usually a wooden table covered with green baize, a three-legged stool, a cupboard, and nails for hat and coat. The rest of the furnishings included "a plain flat-bottom candlestick with iron extinguisher and snuffers, a wooden candle-box, a staff-handle brush, leaden ink-pot, basin and bottle for washing the hands, and a saucer or gallipot for soap." There was always a cotton curtain or a blind before the window. For such a "mansion" the Rugby schoolboy paid from ten to fifteen shillings a year, and the tenant bought his own furniture. *Tom Brown* had a "hard-seated sofa covered with red stuff," big enough to hold two in a "tight squeeze," and he had, besides, a good, stout, wooden chair. Those boys who had mirrors, or looking-glasses as they were called in those days, in their rooms were able to comb their own locks, those who were not so fortunate went to what was known as the "combing-house" and had it done for them.

Unfortunately there are recorded very few details of these school days at Rugby. We can only conjecture, from our knowledge of the boy and his studious ways, that Charles Dodgson's study was his castle, his home, and freehold while he was in the school. He drew around him a circle of friends, for the somewhat sober lad had the gift of talking, and could be jolly and entertaining when he liked.

The chapel at Rugby was an unpretentious Gothic building, very imposing and solemn to little Dodgson, who had been brought up in a most reverential way, but the Rugbeans viewed it in another light. *Tom Brown's* chosen chum explained it to him in this wise:

"That's the chapel you see, and there just behind it is the place for fights; it's most out of the way for masters, who all live on the other side and don't come by here after first lesson or callings-over. That's when the fights come off."

All this must have shocked the simple, law-abiding son of a clergyman. It took from four to six years to tame the average Rugby boy, but little Charles needed no discipline; he was not a "goody-goody" boy, he simply had a natural aversion to rough games and sports. He liked to keep a whole skin, and his mind clear for his studies; he was fond of tramping through the woods, or fishing along the banks of the pretty, winding Avon, or rowing up and down the river, or lying on some grassy slope, still weaving the many odd fancies which grew into clearer shape as the years passed. The boys at Rugby did not know he was a genius, he did not know it himself, happy little lad, just a bit quiet and old-fashioned, for the noisy, blustering life about him. In fact, strange as it may seem, Charles Dodgson was never really a little boy until he was quite grown up.

He easily fell in with the routine of the school, but discipline, even as late as 1846, was hard to maintain. The Headmaster had his hands full; there were six undermasters—one for each form—and special tutors for the boys who required them, and from the fifth and sixth forms, certain monitors were selected called "præposters," (also known as prefects) who were supposed to preserve order among the lower grades.

In reality they bullied the smaller boys, for the system of requiring young pupils to do menial chores for the older pupils was much abused in those days, and the poor little lads had to be bootshiners, water-carriers, and general servants to very hard task-masters, while the "præposter" had little thought of doing any service for the service he exacted; in fact the unfortunate lad had to submit in silence to any indignity inflicted by an older boy, for if by chance a report of such doings came to the ears of the Headmaster or his associates, the talebearer was "sent to Coventry," in other words, he was shunned and left to himself by all his companions.

Injustice like this made little Dodgson's blood boil; he submitted of course with the other small boys, but he always had a peculiar distaste for the life at Rugby. He owned several years later that none of the studying at Rugby was done from real love of it, and he specially bewailed the time he lost in writing out impositions, and he further confessed that under no consideration would he live over those three years again.

These "impositions" were the hundreds of lines of Latin or Greek which the boys had to copy out with their own hands, for the most trifling offenses—a weary and hopeless waste of time, with little good accomplished.

In spite of many drawbacks, he got on finely with his work, seldom returning home for the various holidays without one or more prizes, and we cannot believe that he was quite outside of all the fun and frolic of a

Rugby schoolboy's life. For instance, we may be sure that he went bravely through that terrible ordeal for the newcomer, called "singing in Hall."

"Each new boy," we are told, "was mounted in turn upon a table, a candle in each hand, and told to sing a song. If he made a false note, a violent hiss followed, and during the performance pellets and crusts of bread were thrown at the boy or at the candles, often knocking them out of his hands and covering him with tallow (wax). The singing over, he descended and pledged the house drinking a glass filled to the rim with salt and water, stirred by a tallow candle. He was then free of the house and retired to his room, feeling very uncomfortable."

"On the night after 'new boys' night' there was chorus singing, in which solos and quartets of all sorts were sung, especially old Rugby's favorites such as:
"'It's my delight, on a shiny night
In the season of the year,'
and the proceedings always wound up with 'God save the Queen.'"

Guy Fawkes' Day was another well-known festival at Rugby. There were bonfires in the town, but they were

hISTORY OF
enGLAnD

never kindled until eight o'clock, which was "lock-up" time for Rugby school. The boys resented this as it was great fun and they were out of it, so each year there was a lively scrimmage between the Rugbeans and the town, the former bent on kindling the bonfires before "lock-up" time, the latter doing all they could to hold back the ever-pressing enemy. Victory shifted with the years, from one side to the other, but the boys had their fun all the same, which was over half the battle.

Charles must have gone through Rugby with rapid strides, accomplishing in three years' time what some boys did in eight, and when he left he had the proud distinction of being among the *very* few who had never gone up a certain winding staircase leading, by a small door, into the Master's private presence, where the rod awaited the culprit, and a good heavy rod it was.

During these years Dickens was doing his best work, and while at Rugby, Charles read "David Copperfield," which came out in numbers in the *Penny Magazine*.

He was specially interested in *Mrs. Gummidge*, that mournful, tearful lady, who was constantly bemoaning that she was "a lone lorn creetur," and that everything went "contrairy" with her.

Dickens's humor touched a chord of sympathy in him, and if we go over in our minds, the weeping animals we know in "Alice in Wonderland" and "Through the Looking-Glass," we will find many excellent portraits of *Mrs. Gummidge*.

He also read Macaulay's "History of England," and from it was particularly struck by a passage describing the seven bishops who had signed the invitation to the Pretender. Bishop Compton, one of the seven, when accused by King James, and asked whether he or any of his ecclesiastical brethren had anything to do with it, replied: "I am fully persuaded, your Majesty, that there is not one of my brethren who is not innocent in the matter as myself." This tickled the boy's sense of humor. Those touches always appealed to him; as he grew older they took even a firmer hold upon him and he was quick to pluck a laugh from the heart of things. His life at Rugby was somewhat of a strain; with a brain beginning to teem with a thousand stories and fairytales that the boys around him could not appreciate, he was forced to thrust them out of sight. He flung himself into his studies, coming out at examinations on top in mathematics, Latin, and divinity, and saving that other part of him for his sisters, when he went home for the holidays.

Meantime he continued to write verses and stories and to draw clever caricatures. There is one of these drawings peculiarly Rugbean in character; it is supposed to be a scene in which four of his sisters

are roughly handling a fifth, because she *would* write to her brother when they wished to go to Halnaby and the Castle. This noble effort he signed "Rembrandt." The picture is really very funny. The five girls have very much the appearance of the marionettes he was fond of making, especially the unfortunate correspondent who has been pulled into a horizontal position by the stern sister. The whole story is told by the expression of the eyes and mouth of each, for the clever schoolboy had all the secrets of caricature, without quite enough genius in that direction to make him an artist.

The Rugby days ended in glory; our Boy, no longer little Dodgson, but young Dodgson, came home loaded with honors. Mr. Mayor, his mathematical master, wrote to his father in 1848, that he had never had a more promising boy at his age, since he came to Rugby. Mr. Tait also wrote complimenting him most highly not only for his high standing in mathematics and divinity, but for his conduct while at Rugby, which was all that could be desired.

chapter III.

HOME LIFE DURING THE HOLIDAYS

hen Charles came home on his holiday visits, he was undoubtedly the busiest person at Croft Rectory. We must remember there were ten eager little brothers and sisters who wanted the latest news from "the front," meaning Rugby of course, and Charles found many funny things to tell of the school doings, many exciting matches to recount, many a thrilling adventure, and, alas! many a tale of some popular hero's downfall and disgrace.

He had sketches to show, and verses to read to a most enthusiastic audience, the girls giggling over his funny tales, the boys roaring with excitement as in fancy they pictured the scene at "Big-side" during some great football scrimmage, for Charles's descriptions were so vivid, indeed he was such a good talker always, that a few quaint sentences would throw the whole picture on the canvas.

Vacation time was devoted to literary schemes of all kinds. From little boyhood until he was way up in his "teens," he was the editor of one magazine or another of home manufacture, chiefly, indeed, of his own composition, or drawn from local items of interest to the young people of Croft Rectory. While he was still at Richmond School, *Useful and Instructive Poetry* was born and died in six months' time, and many others shared the same fate; but the young editor was undaunted.

This was the age of small periodicals and he had caught the craze; it was also the age when great genius was burning brightly in England. Tennyson was in his prime; Dickens was writing his stories, and Macaulay his history of England. There were many other geniuses who influenced his later years, Carlyle, Browning and others, but the first three caught his boyish fancy and were his guides during those early days of editorship.

Punch, the great English magazine of wit and humor, attracted him immensely, and many a time his rough drawings caught the spirit of some of the famous cartoons. He never imagined, as he laughed over the broad humor of John Tenniel, that the great cartoonist would one day stand beside him and share the honors of "Alice in Wonderland."

One of his last private efforts in the editorial line was *The Rectory Umbrella*, a magazine undertaken when he was about seventeen or eighteen years old, on the bridge, one might say, between boyhood and his approaching Oxford days. His mind had developed quickly, though his views of life did not go far beyond the rectory grounds.

He evidently took his title out of the umbrella-stand in the rectory hall, the same stand doubtless which furnished him with "The Walking Stick of Destiny," a story of the lurid, exciting sort, which made his readers' hair rise. The magazine also contained a series of sketches supposed to have been copied

from paintings by Rembrandt, Sir Joshua Reynolds and others whose works hang in the Vernon Gallery. One specially funny caricature of Sir Joshua Reynolds's "Age of Innocence" represents a baby hippopotamus smiling serenely under a tree not half big enough to shade him.

Another sketch ridicules homeopathy and is extremely funny. Homeopathy is a branch of medical science which believes in *very* small doses of medicine, and this picture represents housekeeping on a homeopathic plan; a family of six bony specimens are eating minuscule grains of food, which they can only see through the spectacles they all wear, and their table talk hovers round millionths and nonillionths of grains.

age of innocence

But the cleverest poem in *The Rectory Umbrella* is the parody on "Horatius," Macaulay's famous poem, which is supposed to be a true tale of his brothers' adventures with an stubborn donkey. It is the second of the series called "Lays of Sorrow," in imitation of Macaulay's "Lays of Ancient Rome," and the tragedy lies in the sad fact that the donkey succeeds in getting the better of the boys."Horatius" was a great favorite with budding orators of that day. The Rugby boys declaimed it on every occasion, and reading it over in these modern times of peace, one is stirred by the martial note in it. No wonder boys like Charles Dodgson loved Macaulay, and it is pretty safe to say that he must have had it by heart, to have treated it in such spirited style and with such pure fun. Indeed, fun bubbled up through

everything he wrote; wholesome, honest fun, which was a safety valve for an overserious lad.

This period was his halting time, and the humorous skits he dashed off were done in moments of recreation. He was mapping out his future in a methodical way peculiarly his own. Oxford was to be his goal, divinity and mathematics his principal studies, and he was working hard for his examinations. The desire of the eldest son to follow in his father's footsteps was strengthened by his own natural inclination.

Mathematics absorbed many hours of each day, and Latin and Greek were quite as important. English as a "course" was not thought of as it is today; the classics

LORD ALFRED
tennyson

were before everything else, although ancient and modern history came into use. For lighter reading, Dickens was a never-failing source of supply. All during this holiday period "David Copperfield" was coming out in monthly instalments, and though the hero was "only a boy," there was something in the pathetic figure of lonely little *David*, irresistibly appealing to the young fellow who hated oppression and injustice of any kind, and was always on the side of the weak.

While the dainty picture of *Little Em'ly* might have been his favorite, he was keenly alive to the absurdities of *Mrs. Gummidge*, the doglike devotion of *Peggotty*, and the horrors of the "cheap school," which turned out little shivering cowards instead of wholesome hearty English boys.

Later on, he visited the spot on which Dickens had founded *Dotheboys Hall* in "Nicholas Nickleby." "Barnard's Castle" was a most desolate region in Yorkshire. He tells of a trip by coach, over a land of dreary hills, into Bowes, a Godforsaken village where the original of *Dotheboys Hall* was still standing, though in a very dilapidated state, actually falling to pieces.

As we well know, after the writing of "Nicholas Nickleby," government authorities began to look into the condition of the "cheap schools" and to remedy some of the evils. Even the more expensive schools, where the tired little brains were crammed to the brim until the springs were worn out and the minds were gone, were exposed by the great novelist when he wrote "Dombey and Son" and told of *Dr. Blimber's* school, where poor little *Paul* studied until his head grew too heavy for his fragile body and he dies.

But the influence that crept closer to the heart of this boy was that of Tennyson. The great poet with the wonderful dark face, the piercing eyes, the shaggy mane, sending forth clarion messages to the world in waves of song, was the inspiration of many a quaint phrase and poetic turn of thought which later came from the pen of Lewis Carroll. Meanwhile, young Charles Dodgson read his poems over and over, in the seclusion of Croft Rectory, during that quiet pause in his life before he went up to Oxford.

There was a village school of some importance in Croft, and members of the Dodgson family were interested in its welfare, often lending a hand with the teaching, and during those months, no doubt, Charles took his turn. For society, his own family seemed to be sufficient. Indeed, the only friend mentioned is T. Vere Bayne, who in childish days was his playfellow and who later became, like himself, a Student of Christ Church. This association cemented a lasting friendship.

Walking was always a favorite pastime; the woods were full of the things he loved. Its creatures became real companions in time. He studied their ways and habits, he looked them up in the Natural History, and noting their peculiarities, tucked them away in that quaint cupboard of his which he called his memory. How many things were to come out of that cupboard in later days!

chRist chuRch

So, through a long vista of years, we have the picture of our Boy, between eighteen and nineteen, when he was about to put boyhood by forever and enter the stately ranks of the Oxford undergraduates. As he stands before us now, young, ardent, hopeful, and inexperienced, we can see no glimmer of the fairy wand which turned him into a wizard.

We see only a boy, somewhat old for his years, very manly in his ways, with a well-formed head, on which the clustering dark hair grew thick; a sensitive mouth and deep blue eyes, full of expression. He was clever, imitative, and consequently a good actor in the little plays he wrote and dramatized; he was very shy, but at his best in the home circle. He enjoyed nothing so much as an argument, always holding his ground with great obstinacy; a fine student, frank and affectionate, brimful of wit and humor, fond of reading, with a quiet determination to excel in whatever he undertook. With such weapons he was

well equipped to "storm the citadel" at Oxford.

On May 23, 1850, he went up to matriculate—that is, to register his name and go through some examinations and the formality of becoming a student. Christ Church was to be his college, as it had been his father's before him. Archdeacon Dodgson was much gratified by the many letters he received congratulating him on the fact that he had a son worthy to succeed him, for he was well remembered in the college, where he had left a brilliant record behind him.

It certainly sounds a little strange to have the name of a church attached to one of the colleges of a university, but our colleges in America are comparatively so new that we cannot grasp the vastness and the antiquity of the great English universities. Under the shelter of Oxford, and covering an area of at least five miles, twenty colleges or more were grouped, each one a community in itself, and all under the rule of the Chancellor of Oxford. Christ Church received as students those most interested in the divinity courses, though in other respects the undergraduates could take up whatever studies they pleased, and Charles Dodgson put most of his energy into mathematics and the necessary study of the classics.

chapter IV.

OXFORD SCHOLAR- SHIP AND HONORS

n January 24, 1851, just three days before his nineteenth birthday, Charles Dodgson took up his residence at Christ Church, and from that time to the day of his death his name was always associated with the fine old building which was his *Alma Mater*.

The men of Christ Church called it the "House," and were very proud of their college, as well they might be, for Oxford could not boast of a more imposing structure. There is a great difference between a university and a college. A university is great enough to shelter many colleges, and its chancellor is ruler over all. When we reflect that Christ Church College, alone, included as many important buildings as are to be found in some of our modern American universities, we may have some idea of the extent of Oxford University, within whose boundaries twenty such colleges could be counted.

Their names were all familiar to the young fellow, and many a time, in those early days, he could be found in his boat upon the river, floating gently down stream, the whole panorama of Oxford spread out before him.

The spire of St. Aldates (pronounced St. Olds); Sir Christopher Wren's domed tower over the entrance to Christ Church; the spires of the Cathedral of St. Mary; the tower of All Saints; the twin towers of All Souls; the dome of Radcliffe Library; the massive tower of Merton, and the beautiful pinnacles of Magdalen, all passed before him.

History springs up with every step one takes in Oxford. The University can trace its origin to the time of Alfred the Great. Beginning with only three colleges, each year this great center of learning became more important. Henry I built the Palace of Beaumont at Oxford, because he wished frequent opportunities to talk with men of learning. It was from the Castle of Oxford that the Empress Maud escaped at dead of night, in a white gown, over the snow and the frozen river, when Stephen usurped the throne. It was in the Palace of Beaumont that Richard the Lion-Hearted was born, and so on, through the centuries, great deeds and great events could be traced to the very gates of Oxford.

Christ Church really owes its foundation to the famous Cardinal Wolsey. Charles Lutwidge Dodgson knew its history by heart; how the wicked old Cardinal, wishing to leave behind him a monument of lasting good to cover his many misdeeds, obtained the royal license to found the college as early as 1525; how, in 1529, as Shakespeare said, he bade "a long farewell to all his greatness," and his possessions, including Cardinal College as it was then called, fell into the ruthless hands of Henry VIII; and how, after many ups and downs, the present foundation of Christ Church was created under "letters patent of Henry VIII dated November 4, 1546."

Christ Church, with its imposing front of four hundred feet, is built around the Great Quadrangle, quite famous in the history of the college. It includes in the embrace of its four sides the library and picture gallery, the Cathedral and the Chapter House, and the homes of the dean and his associates. There was another smaller quadrangle called Peckwater Quadrangle, where young Dodgson had his rooms when he first entered college, but later when he became a tutor or a "don" as the instructors were usually called, he moved into the Great Quadrangle.

A beautiful meadow lies beyond the south gate, spreading out in a long and fertile stretch to the river's edge. The massive front gate has towers and turrets on either side, while just above it is the great "Tom Tower," the present home of "Tom" the famous bell, measuring over seven feet in diameter and weighing over seven tons.

This bell was originally dedicated to St. Thomas of Canterbury, and bore a Latin inscription in praise of the saint. It was brought from the famous Abbey of Oseney, when that cloister was transferred to Oxford, and on the accession of Queen Mary. It

henry viii

rang first in it's actual tower on the anniversary of the Restoration, May 29, 1684, and since then has rung each morning and evening, at the opening and closing of the college gates.

"Tom Tower," as it is called, overlooks that portion of the Great Quadrangle popularly known as "Tom Quad," and it was in this corner of the Great Quadrangle that Lewis Carroll had his rooms. He speaks of it often in his many reminiscences, as he also spoke of the new bell tower over the hall staircase in the southeast corner.

cardinal wolsey

Young Dodgson went into his studies, as he did into everything else, with his whole soul. He devoted a great deal of his time to mathematics, and quite as much to divinity, but just as he had settled down for months of serious work, the news of his mother's sudden death sent him hurrying back to Croft Rectory to join the sorrowing household.

It was a terrible blow to them all; with this young family growing up around her, she could ill be spared, and the loss of her filled those first Oxford days with dark shadows for the boy — he was only a boy still for all his nineteen years — and we can imagine how deeply he mourned for his mother. What we know of her is very faint and shadowy. That her influence was keenly felt for many years, we can only glean from the love and reverence with which the memory of her was guarded; for this English home hid its grief in the depths of its heart, and only the privileged few might enter and

console. This was the first and only break in the family for many years. Charles went back to Oxford immediately after the funeral, and took up his studies again with redoubled zeal.

Thomas Gaisford was dean of Christ Church during the four years that Charles Dodgson was an undergraduate. He was a most able man, well known as scholar, writer, and thinker, but he died, much lamented, in 1855, just as the young student was thinking seriously of a life devoted to his college. George Henry Liddell came into residence as dean of Christ Church, an office which he held for nearly forty years, and as Dean Liddell stood for a great deal in the life of Charles Dodgson, we shall hear much of him from time to time, dating more especially from the comradeship of his three little daughters.

But we are jumping over too many years at once, and must go back a few steps. His hard study during the first year won him a Boulter scholarship; the next year he took First Class honors in mathematics, and a second in classical studies, and on Christmas Eve, 1852, he was made a Student of Christ Church College.

To become a Student of Christ Church was not only a great honor, conferred only on one altogether worthy of it, but it was a very serious step in life for a young man. From that time forth he ordered his life as he planned his mathematics, clearly and simply, and once his career was settled, Charles Lutwidge Dodgson dropped from his young shoulders—he was only twenty—the mantle of over-seriousness, and looked about for some entertainment.

He started walking about the huge Campus, row his boat down the river and occassionally went to see a play. But his greatest pleasure was to make the masters and the tutors' kids laugh. Their homes looked out upon the Great Quadrangle and here on sunny days the nannys brought the children for an airing. His slim figure in cap and gown when he arrived from a day's work caught the attention of the children one day and they surrounded him and asked him a lot of questions. He in return told them stories of the animals he knew, and drew funny little pictures on stray bits of paper. After that, it became a tradition. His coming was always hailed with delight.

Sometimes he would accompanied them for a stroll,
where he spun story after story for them in his
quaint way, filling their little heads with odd fancies
which would never have been there but for him. The
"bunnies" held animated conversations with these
small maids; every chirp and twitter of the birds
grew to mean something to them. He took them
across the meadow, and showed them the turtles
swimming on the river bank; sometimes even—oh,
treat of treats!—he took them in his boat, and
pulling gently down the pretty rippling stream, told
them stories of the shining fish they could see
darting here and there in its depths, and of
wonderful creatures they could *not* see, who would
not show themselves while curious little kids were
staring into the water.

These were hours of pure recreation for him. Athletics never appealed to him, even boating he enjoyed in his own mild way; a quiet pull up or down the river, a shady bank, an hour's rest under the trees—this was what he liked best. On other days a tramp of miles gave just the exercise he needed.

His busy day began at a quarter past six, with breakfast at seven, and chapel at eight. Then came the day's lectures in Greek and Latin, mathematics, divinity, and the classics. Meals were served to the undergraduates in the Hall. The men were divided into "messes" just as in military posts; each "mess" consisted of about six men, who were served at a small table. There were many such tables scattered

BOAT RACE AT OXFORD

over the Hall, a vast and ancient room, completed at the time of Wolsey's fall, 1529, an interesting spot full of memorials of Henry VIII and Wolsey.

The great west window with its two rows of shields, some with a Cardinal's hat, others with the royal arms of Henry VIII, is most interesting, while the wainscoting, decorated with shields also arranged in orderly fashion, is very attractive. The Hall is filled with portraits of celebrities, from Henry VIII, Wolsey and Elizabeth to the many students, and famous deans, who have added luster to Christ Church.

In Charles Dodgson's time, the meals were poorly served. The Hall was lighted at night with candles in brass candlesticks made to hold three lights each. The undergraduates were served on pewter plates, and the poor young fellows were in the hands of the cook and butler, and consequently were cheated up to their eyes.

They did not complain in Charles Dodgson's time, but after he graduated and became a master himself he no doubt took part in what was known as the "Bread and Butter" campaign, when the undergraduates rose up in a body and settled the cook and butler for all time, appointing a steward who could overlook the doings of those below in the kitchen.

This kitchen is a very wonderful old place, the first portion of Wolsey's work to be completed, and so strongly was it built, and so well has it lasted, that it seems scarcely to have been touched by time. Of course there are some modern improvements, but the great ranges are still there, and the wide fireplace and spits worked by a "smoke jack." Wolsey's own gridiron hangs just above the fireplace, a large uncouth broiler, fit for cooking the huge hunks of meat the Cardinal liked best.

We must not imagine that the years at Oxford were "all work and no play," for Charles Dodgson's many vacations were spent either at home, where his father made much of him, his brothers looked up to him, and his sisters petted and spoiled him, or on little trips of interest and amusement.

Once, during what is known as the "Long Vacation," he visited London at the time of the Great Exhibition, and wrote a vivid letter of description to his sister Elizabeth. What seemed to interest him most was the vastness of everything he saw, the huge crystal fountain and the colossal

GREAT EXHIBITION

statues on either side of the central aisle. One statue he particularly noticed. It was called the "Amazon and the Tiger," and many of us have doubtless seen the picture, the strong, erect, girlish figure on horseback, and the tiger clinging to the horse, his teeth buried in his neck, the girl's face full of terror, the horse rearing with fright and pain.

He always liked anything that told a story, either in statues or in pictures, and in after years, when he became a skilled photographer, he was fond of taking pictures of his friends in costume, representing popular characters, for somehow it always suggested a story.

He was also very fond of the theater, and he made many trips to London to see a play. Shakespeare was his delight, and "Henry VIII" was certainly the most appropriate play for a Student of Christ Church College to see. The great actor, Charles Kean, took the part of *Cardinal Wolsey*, and Mrs. Kean shone forth as poor *Queen Katharine*, the discarded wife of Henry VIII. What impressed him most was the vision of the sleeping queen, the troops of floating angels with palm branches in their hands, which they waved slowly over her, while shafts of light fell upon them from above. Then as the Queen awoke they vanished,

and raising her arms she called "Spirits of peace, where are ye?" Poor Queen, no wonder her audience shed tears! Henry VIII was not an easy man to get along with, even in his sweetest mood!

In 1854, Charles Dodgson began hard study for final examinations, working sometimes as many as thirteen hours a day during the last three weeks, but the subjects which he had to prepare were philosophy and history, neither of which were special favorites, and though he passed fairly well, his name was not among the first.

OXFORD
UNIVERSITY PRESS

During the following Long Vacation he went to Whitby, where he prepared for final examination in mathematics, and so well did he work that he took First Class honors and became quite a distinguished personage among the undergraduates. His prowess in so difficult a subject traveled even beyond the college walls, and congratulations poured in upon him until he laughingly declared that if he had shot the Dean there could not have been more commotion.

This meant a great deal to him; to begin with, he stood head on the list of five very able men who were close to him in the marking. He came out number 279 and the lowest of the five was 213, so it was a hard fight in a hard subject, and Lewis Carroll might be forgiven for a little quiet "bragging" in the letter he wrote his father, telling the result of the examinations. Of one thing he was now quite sure—a future lectureship in Christ Church College. On December 18, 1854, he graduated, taking the degree of Bachelor of Arts, and the following year, October 15, 1855, to celebrate the appointment of Dean Liddell, he was made a "Master of the House," meaning that under the roof of Christ Church College he had all the privileges of a Master of Arts, which is the next higher degree; but he did not become a Master of Arts in the University until two years later. When a college graduate puts B.A. after his name, we know that means Bachelor of Arts, the first college degree, and M.A. means Master of Arts, the second degree.

The young Student was glad to be free of college restraint and to begin work. Archdeacon Dodgson was not a rich man, and though his son had never faced the trials of poverty, he was anxious to become independent. Now that the "grinding" study was over, his thoughts turned fondly to a literary life.

His numerous clever sketches, too, gave him hope of better work hereafter, and this we know had been his dream through his boyish years; it was his dream still, but where his talent would lie he had no idea, though hazy poems and queer jumbles of words popped into his mind on the slightest notice. Still he could not settle down seriously to such work just at first; there was other work at hand and he must learn to wait.

During the first year of tutorship he took many private pupils, besides lecturing in mathematics, his chosen profession, from three to three and a half hours a day. The next year he was one of the regular lecturers, and often lectured seven hours a day, not counting the time it took him to prepare his work.

Mathematicians are born, not made; this young fellow had not only the power of solving problems, but the rare gift of being able to teach others to solve

CROFT RECTORY

them also, and many a student has been heard to declare that mathematics was never a dull study with Mr. Dodgson to explain. He "took to" problems as naturally as a duck to water; the harder they were the more resolutely he bent to his task. Sometimes the tussle kept him awake half the night, often he was up at dawn to renew the battle, but he usually "won out," and this is what made him so good a teacher— he *never* "let go." Whatever mathematical ax he had to grind, he always managed to put a keen edge upon it sooner or later. To his many friends this side of his character was most remarkable. How this fun-making, fun-loving, story-telling nonsense rhymer could turn in a twinkling into the grave, precise "don" and discourse on rectangles, and polygons, and parallel lines, and unknown quantities was more than they could understand.

So the years passed over the head of this young Student of Christ Church. They were pleasantly broken by long vacations at Croft Rectory, by trips through the beautiful English country, by one special journey to the English lakes, where Wordsworth, Southey, and Coleridge lived and wrote their poems. These trips were often afoot, and Charles Dodgson was very proud of the long distances he could tramp, no matter what the wind or the weather. There was nothing he liked better unless it was the occasional visits he made to the Princess's Theatre in London.

On June 16, 1856, he records seeing "A Winter's Tale," where he was specially pleased with young Ellen Terry, a beautiful tiny creature, who played the child's part of *Mamillius* in the most charming way. This was the first of many meetings with the famous actress, who became one of his friends in later years. But that was when he was Lewis Carroll.

ellen terry and
the winter's tale

chapter v.

A MANY-SIDED GENIUS

e have traveled over the years with some speed, from the time that little Charles Lutwidge Dodgson waste christened by his proud papa to the moment when the same proud father heard that his eldest son was made a student of Christ College —a good large slice out of a birthday-cake—twenty candles—if one counts birthdays by candles.

We have just passed over the very oldest part of our Boy's life, because, you see, so far he had behave as a very mature older person. He had been so serious and studious as a boy, that once he became Lewis Carroll, he embraced all the stories and fancies in his head, let his imagination loose, started to enjoy life more and dedicated his efforts for the entertainment of children, as if he had turned backwards to find the boyhood he had somehow missed before. So we can say that from the time he became Lewis Carroll, Charles Dodgson began to live backward; and he did a lot of things backward later in life. He wrote letters backward to his friends, he told stories backward, he spelled and counted backward. This is when Lewis Carroll was born; but that is a story in itself.

Outwardly the life of the young student seemed unchanged, but that is all we mortals know about it; the fairies were already at work. In moments of leisure little poems went forth to the world—a world which at first consisted of Croft Rectory—for there was another and last family magazine, of which he was sole editor and composer. He named it *Misch-Masch*, a curious old German word, which in our English means Hodge-Podge -a stew made from meat and vegetables- and everybody, young and old, knows what a jumble Hodge-Podge is.

Misch-Masch was started by this enterprising young editor during the year after his graduation. He had become a person of vast experience having been editor of *College Rhymes*, his college paper.

For his little magazine he wrote stories, with many new and original ideas and drawings. He also included wonderful mazes and

ꝺoꝺɢꑀon 걞eꝇꝼ~portrait

puzzles. One specially good drawing was from a series he wrote called "Studies from the English Poets, which he illustrated himself, where an old lady was perched on a post marked "Dangerous", seemingly in midwater.

Misch-Masch had a short but brilliant career, for magazines with a wider circulation began to claim his attention. *The Comic Times* was a small periodical very much on the order of *Punch*. Edmund Yates was the editor, and among the writers and artists were some of the best known in England. Charles Dodgson's poetry and sketches were too clever to hide themselves from public view, and he became a regular contributor.

Later, *The Comic Times* changed hands, and the old staff started a new magazine called *The Train*, in 1856, and the quiet Oxford "don" found his poetry in such demand that after talking it over with the editor, he decided to adopt a suitable pen name. He first suggested "Dares" in compliment to his birthplace, Daresbury, but the editor preferred a *real* name. Then he took his first two names, Charles Lutwidge, and transposing them he got two names, Edgar Cuthwellis or Edgar U. C. Westhill, neither of which sounded in the least interesting. Finally he decided to take the two names and look at them backward—this very queer young fellow always preferred to look at things backward—Lutwidge Charles. That was certainly not promising. Then he took one name at a time and analyzed it in his own quaint way. Lutwidge was surely derived from the Latin word Ludovicus—which in good sound English meant Lewis—ah, that was not bad! Now for Charles. Its Latin equivalent was Carolus—which could be easily changed in Carroll. The whole thing worked out like one of his own word puzzles, and Lewis Carroll he was, henceforth, whenever he made his appearance in print.

There was not much ceremony at *this* christening. Just two clever men put their heads together and the result was—Lewis Carroll! Charles Lutwidge Dodgson retired to his rooms at Christ Church College, where he prepared his lectures on mathematics and wrote the most learned textbooks for the University; but Lewis Carroll peeped out into the world, which he found full of light and laughter and happy childhood, and as Lewis Carroll he was known to that world henceforth.

The first poem to appear with his new name was called "The Path of Roses," a very solemn, serious poem about half a yard long and not specially interesting, save as a contribution to a most interesting little paper. *The Train* was really very ambitious, full, indeed, of the best talent of the day. There were short stories and serials, poems, timely articles, jokes, puns, anecdates—in short, all the attractions that help toward the making of an attractive magazine, and though the illustrations were nothing but old-fashioned woodcuts, the reading was quite as good, and in many cases better than what we find in the average magazine of today.

In his secret soul he longed to be an artist; he certainly possessed genius of a peculiar sort. A few strokes would tell the story, usually a funny one or a quaint one, but all his art failed to make his people look quite real or natural—just dolls stuffed with sawdust. But they were   fine caricatures, and the

young artist had to content himself with this smaller talent.

The Train published many of his poems during 1856-57. "Solitude," "Novelty and Romancement," "The Three Voices," followed one another in quick succession, but the best of all was decidedly "Hiawatha's Photographing," and this for more reasons than one. In the first place, from the time he went into residence at Christ Church photography was his great delight; he took photos of people whenever he could—canons, deacons, deans, students, undergraduates and children.

The "grown-ups" submitted with a gentle sort of patience, but he made his camera such a point of attraction for the youngsters that he could take their photographs as often as he liked, and he left behind him a wonderful array of photographs, many of well-known, even celebrated people, among whom we may find Tennyson, the Rossetti family, Ellen and Kate Terry, John Ruskin, George Macdonald, Charlotte M. Yonge, Sir John Millais, and many others known to fame; and considering that photography had not reached its present perfection, Lewis Carroll's photographs show remarkable skill. He would not have been Lewis Carroll if he had not gone into this fascinating pastime with his whole soul. Whenever he met a new face which interested him, we may be sure it was not long before the busy camera was at work. There is no doubt that his admiring family suffered agonies in posing, to say nothing of his friends who were not always beautiful enough to produce "pretty pictures".

The year 1858 was an uneventful year; college routine varied by much reading, afternoons on the river or in the country, and evenings devoted to preparations for

LORD tennyson and young dodgson in photos taken by himself

tomorrow's work. Lewis Carroll kept a diary which harbored many fine thoughts and noble resolves, many doubts and fears, many hopes, many plans for the future. But what he could not predict was that soon he would be in the company of Royalty.

On October 17, 1859, the young Prince of Wales (the late King Edward VII) came into residence at Christ Church College. This was a mark of special favor to Dean Liddell, who had for many years been chaplain to Queen Victoria and her husband, the Prince Consort. Of course there was much ceremony attending the arrival of his Royal Highness; the Dean went in person to the station to meet him, and all the "dons" were drawn up in a body in Tom Quadrangle to give him the proper sort of greeting. Charles had his camera along— but "in its case it lay compactly," because the young Highness had been "served up" on the camera to his utter disgust, and nothing would induce him to be photographed.

Later in the season, the Queen, the Prince Consort, and several princes and princesses came up to Oxford and surprised everybody. Christ Church was certainly in a flutter, and the day was turned into a gala occasion. There was a brilliant reception that evening at Dean Liddell's house including the making of *tableaux vivants*, or "living pictures", where a silent and motionless group of people arranged to represent a book scene or an incident who had made the news, to which we may be sure our modest Lewis Carroll gave much assistance. He was already on friendly terms with the three little Liddells, Lorina, Alice, and Edith, and as the children were to pose in a

the prince of wales went to oxford

tableau, he was there to help and suggest with a score of quaint ideas.

He had a pleasant talk with the Prince of Wales, who shook hands cordially and condescended to ask several questions of the young photographer, praising the photographs which he had seen, and promised to choose some for himself some day. As a result of his interview with the prince, Lewis Carroll obtained his autograph, which was quite a gem among his collection.

On December 22, 1861, Charles Dodgson was ordained deacon by the Bishop of Oxford. He did this partly from his duty as a Student of Christ Church, but more because of the influence it would give him among the undergraduates, whose welfare he had so much at heart. He preached often but he never became a regular officiating clergyman, and his sermons were always delightful because they were never what we call "preachy." Such was the character of Lewis Carroll up to the year 1862, that momentous year in which he found the golden key of Fairyland.

So far, he had succeeded beyond his hopes in his efforts for independence; he was establishing a brilliant record as a mathematical lecturer; he had several scholarships which paid him a small yearly sum, and he was also sublibrarian. His little poems were making their way into public notice and his more serious work had been mathematic textbooks for Geometry, Trigonometry and Algebra.

Socially, sometimes he had tea with Dean Liddell's family or went for a stroll with them, for Oxford had many beautiful walks about her colleges. The bright companionship of the Liddell girls brought forth the many sides of his genius; under the spell of their winsome chatter the long golden afternoon would glide happily by, while under his spell they would sit for hours listening to the wonder tales he spun for them.

his study at Oxford

chapter VI.

DOWN THE RIVER WITH THE REAL ALICE

e generally speak of Oxford-on-the-Thames. Indeed, if we were to journey by water from London to Oxford, we would certainly go by way of the river Thames, and a pleasant journey that would be, too, gliding between well-wooded, fertile shores with charming landscape towns on either side and bits of history peeping out in unexpected places. But into the heart of Oxford itself the Thames sends forth its tributaries in opposite directions; the Isis on one side, the Cherwell on the other. The Cherwell is what is called a "canoe river," the Isis is the race course of Oxford, where all the "eights" (every racing crew consists of eight men) come to practice for the great day and the great race, which takes place sometimes at Henley, sometimes at Oxford itself, when the Isis's bank is full with bunting and flags.

On one side of Christ Church Meadow was a long line of barges which were made stationary and which were used as boathouses by the various college clubs; these were situated just below what is known as Folly Bridge, a name familiar to all Oxford men, and the goal of many pleasant trips.

The original bridge was destroyed in 1779, but tradition tells us that the first bridge was capped by a tower which was the study or observatory of Roger Bacon, the Franciscan Friar who invented the telescope, gunpowder, and many other things unknown to the people of his time. It was even hinted that he had cunningly built this tower that it might fall instantly on anyone passing beneath it who proved to be more learned than himself.

One could see it from Christ Church Meadow, and doubtless Lewis Carroll pointed it out to his small companions, as they strolled across to the water's edge, where perhaps a boat rocked lazily at its moorings. It was the work of a moment to steady it so that the eager youngsters could scramble in, then he stepped in himself, pushing off with his oar, and a few long, steady strokes brought them in midstream.

This was an ordinary afternoon occurrence, and the children alone knew the delights of being the chosen companions of Lewis Carroll. He would let them row, while he would lounge among the cushions and "spin yarns" that brought peals of merry laughter that rippled over the surface of the water. He knew by heart every story and tradition of

Oxford, from the time the Romans reduced it from a city of some importance to a mere "ford for oxen to pass over," which, indeed, was the origin of its name, long before the Christian era.

He had a story or a legend about every place they passed, but most of all they loved the stories he "made up" as he went along. He had a low, well-pitched voice, with the delightful trick of dropping it in moments of profound interest, sometimes stopping altogether and closing his eyes in pretended sleep, when his listeners were truly thrilled. This, of course, produced a stampede, which he enjoyed immensely, and sometimes he would "wake up," take the oars himself, and pull for some green shady nook that loomed invitingly in the distance; here they would land and under the friendly trees they would have their tea, and

then they *might* induce him to finish the story—if
they were *ever* so good.

It was on just such an occasion that he chanced to
find the golden key to Wonderland. The time was
midsummer, the place on the way up the river
toward Godstow Bridge; the company consisted of
three winsome little girls, Lorina, Alice, and Edith
Liddell, or *Prima*, *Secunda*, and *Tertia*, as he called
them by number in Latin in the order of their birth.

It was the fourth of July, 1862, that this special little
picnic party set out for its trip up the river. They
landed in a cool, green meadow and took refuge
under a hayrick. Lewis Carroll stretched himself out
at full length in the protecting shade, while the
expectant little girls grouped themselves about him.

"Now begin it," demanded Lorina, who was called
Prima. *Secunda* [Alice] probably knew the story-
teller pretty well when she asked for nonsense,
while tiny *Tertia*, the youngest, simply clamored for
"more, more, more," as the speaker's breath gave
out.

Now, as Lewis Carroll lay there, a thousand odd
fancies elbowing one another in his active brain, his
hands groping in the soft moist earth about him, his

fingers suddenly closed over that magic Golden
Key. It was a queer invisible key, just the kind that
fairies use, and neither
Lorina, Alice, nor Edith
would have been able to
find it if they had hunted
ever so long.   Perhaps
there   was   a   door
somewhere that the key
might fit; but no, there was
only the hayrick towering
above him, and only the
brown earth stretching all
about him. Perhaps a
white rabbit *did* whisk by,
perhaps the real Alice
really fell asleep, at any
rate when *Prima* said
"Begin it," that is how he
started.

The Golden Key opened
the brown earth—in
popped the white rabbit—
down dropped the
sleeping Alice—down—
down—down—and while

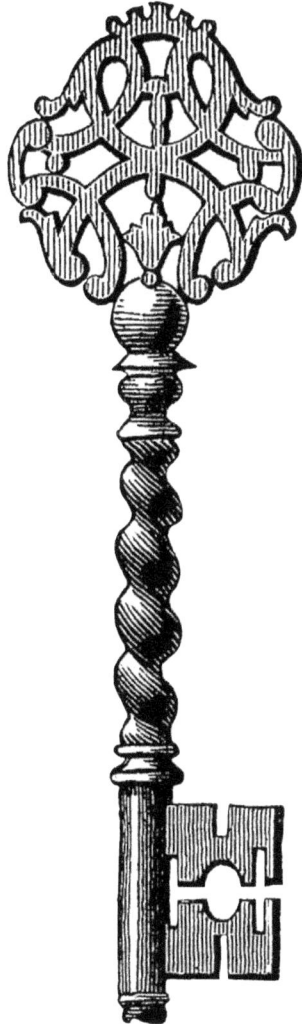

she was falling, clutching at things on the way, Lewis Carroll turned, with one of his rare sweet smiles, to the eager trio and began the story of "Alice's Adventures Underground."

The whole of that long afternoon he held the children spellbound. He did not finish the story during that one sitting. Summer has many long days, and the quiet, prudent young "don" was not reckless enough to scatter *all* his treasures at once; and, besides, all the queer things that happened to Alice would have lost half their interest in the

ORIGINAL handwRITTEN manuscRIpt

shadow of a hayrick, and how could one conjure up *Mock Turtles* and *Lorys* and *Gryphons* on the dry land?

Lewis Carroll's own recollection of the beginning of "Alice" is certainly dated from that "golden afternoon" in the boat, and any idea of publishing the web of nonsense he was weaving never crossed his mind. Indeed, if he could have imagined that his small audience of three would grow to be as many millions in the years to come, the book would have lost half its charm, and the real child that lay hidden under the cap and gown of this grave young Student of thirty might never have been known to the world.

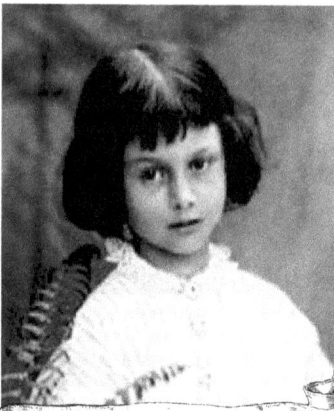

aLICE LIddeLL
the ReaL aLICE

Into his mind, with all the freshness of unbidden thought, popped this story of *Alice* and her strange adventures, and while he chose the name of Alice in seeming carelessness, there is no doubt that the little maid who originally owned the name had many points in common with the protagonist of his most famous story.

To begin with, the real Alice had an Imagination; any child who demands nonsense in a story has an Imagination. Nothing was too impossible or absurd to put into a story, for one could always "make believe" it was something else you see, and a constant "make believe" made everything seem quite real. Lewis Carroll could not help being just the *least* bit partial to Alice, because, as he himself might have quaintly expressed it, she understood everything he said, even before he said it.

She was a dear   little round, chubby child, a great camera favorite, for he took her picture on all occasions. One, as a beggar child, has become quite famous. She is pictured standing, with her ragged dress slipping from her shoulders and her right hand held as if begging for pennies; the other hand rests upon her hip, and her head is bent in a meek fashion; but the mouth has a roguish curve, and there is just the shadow of a laugh in the dark eyes, for of course it's only "make believe," and no one knows it better than Alice herself.

At any rate, if it hadn't been for Alice there would have been no Wonderland, and without Wonderland, childhood is but a tale half-told, and even to this day, every little girl bearing the name of Alice who has read the book and has anything of an imagination, firmly believes that *she* is the sole and only Alice who could venture into Lewis Carroll's Wonderland.

After he had told the story and the original Alice had expressed her approval, he promised to write it out for her to keep. Of course this took time, because, in the first place, his writing was not quite plain enough for a child to read easily, so every letter was carefully printed. Then the illustrations were troublesome, and he drew as many as he could, consulting a book on natural history for the correct forms of the queer animals *Alice* found. The *Mock Turtle* was his own invention, for there never *was* such an animal on land or sea.

This book was handed over to the small Alice, who little dreamed at that time of the treasure she was to have in her keeping. Over twenty years later, when Alice had become Mrs. Reginald Hargreaves, the great popularity of "Alice in Wonderland" tempted the publishers to bring out a reproduction of the original manuscript. This could not be done without borrowing the precious volume from the original Alice, who was willing to trust it in the hands of her

old friend, knowing how over-careful he would be, and, as he resolved that he would not allow any workman to touch it, he had some funny experiences.

To reproduce a book it must first be photographed, and of course Lewis Carroll consulted an expert. He offered to bring the book to London, to go daily to his studio and hold it in position to be photographed, turning over the pages one by one, but the photographer wished to do all that himself. Finally, a man was found who was willing to come to Oxford and do the work in Lewis Carroll's own way, while he stood near by turning over the pages himself rather than let him touch them.

The photographer succeeded in getting a fine set of negatives, and in October, 1880, Lewis Carroll sent the book in safe custody back to its owner, thinking his troubles were over. The next step was to have plates made from the pictures, and these plates in turn could pass into print. The photographer was prompt at first in delivering the plates as they were made, but, finally, he suddenly vanished away, holding still twenty-two of the fine blocks on which the plates were made, leaving the book so far— incomplete.

There ensued a lively search for the missing photographer. This lasted for months, thereby delaying the publication of the book, which was due Christmas. Then, as suddenly as he had disappeared, he reappeared like a ghost at the publishers, left eight of the twenty-two zinc blocks, and again vanished. Finally, when a year had passed and poor Lewis Carroll, at his wits' end, had resolved to borrow the book again in order to photograph the remaining fourteen pages, the man was frightened by threats of arrest, and delivered up the fourteen negatives which he had not yet transferred to the blocks.

SIR John tenniel
cartoonist

The distracted author was glad to find them, even though he had to pay a second time for getting the blocks done properly. However, the book was finished in time for the Christmas sale of 1886, just twenty-one years after "Alice" made her first bow, and the best thing about it was that all the profits were given to the Children's Hospitals and Convalescent Homes for Sick Children. It was thoroughly illustrated with thirty-seven of the author's own drawings, and the grown-up "Alice" received a beautiful special copy bound in white vellum; but pretty as it was, it could not take the place of that other volume carefully written out for the sole pleasure of one little girl.

To go back to the little Alice and the fair smiling river, and that wizard Lewis Carroll, who told the wonder tales so long ago. When he presented the promised copy it might have passed forever from his mind, which was full of the higher mathematics he was teaching to the young men of Christ Church, but he chanced one day to show the manuscript to George Macdonald, the well-known writer, who was so charmed with it that he advised his friend to send it to a publisher. He accordingly carried it to London, and Macmillan & Co. took it at once. This was a great surprise.

He never dreamed of his nonsense being considered seriously, and growing suddenly bashful, he refused to allow his own rough illustrations to appear in print, so he hunted over the long list of his artist friends, for the one who could best illustrate the adventures of his dream-child. At last his friend, Tom Taylor, a well-known dramatist, suggested Mr. Tenniel, the clever cartoonist for *Punch*, who was quite willing to undertake this rather odd bit of work, and on July 4, 1865, exactly three years since that

memorable afternoon, Alice Liddell received the first printed copy of "Alice in Wonderland," the name the author finally selected for his book.

His first idea, as we know, was "Alice's Adventures Underground," the second was "Alice's Hour in Elfland," but the last seemed best of all, for Wonderland might mean any place where wonderful things could happen. And this was Lewis Carroll's idea; anywhere the dream "Alice" chose to go

would be Wonderland, and none knew better than he did how eagerly the child-mind paints its own fairy nooks and corners.

He was not at all excited about his first big venture. To feel that you are about to be put into print is certainly a great experience, almost as great as being photographed; but, knowing how conscientious Lewis Carroll was about little things, we may be quite sure he was more worried than excited.

The first edition of two thousand copies was a great disappointment; the pictures were badly printed, and all who had bought them were asked to send them back with their names and addresses, as a new edition would be printed immediately and they would then receive perfect copies. The old copies Lewis Carroll gave away to various homes and hospitals, while the new edition, upon which he feared a great loss, sold so rapidly that he was astonished, and still more so when edition after edition was demanded by the public, and far from being a failure, "Alice in Wonderland" brought her author both fame and money.

Of course, everyone knew that a certain Lewis Carroll had written a clever, charming book of nonsense, called "Alice in Wonderland"; that he was an Oxford man, very much of a scholar, and little known outside of the University. What people did not know was that this same Lewis Carroll had for a double a certain "grave and reverend" young "don," named Charles Lutwidge Dodgson, who, while "Alice" was making the whole world laugh, retired to his sanctum and wrote in rapid succession five more mathematical treatises and textbooks.

A funny tale is told about Queen Victoria. It seems that Lewis Carroll sent the second presentation copy of "Alice in Wonderland" to Princess Beatrice, the Queen's youngest daughter. Her mother was so pleased with the book that she asked to have the author's other works   sent to her, and we can imagine her surprise when she received a large package of learned treatises by the mathematical lecturer of Christ Church College.

queen
victoria

chapter VII.

CONCLUSION

CONCLUSION

All true fame is to a certain extent due to accident; an act of heroism is generally performed on the spur of the moment; a great poem is an inspiration; a great invention, though preceded possibly by years of study, is born of a single moment's inspiration; so "Alice" came to Lewis Carroll on the wings of inspiration.

The beauty of Lewis Carroll's "nonsense" was that he never tried to be funny or "smart." The queer words and the still queerer ideas popped into his head in the simplest way. To children it is one big fairy tale where the more ridiculous the situations, the more true to the rules of fairyland. But we know from experience that Lewis Carroll's nonsense was not stupidity, and that not one verse in all that delightful bundle missed its own special meaning and purpose.

We do not propose to find the key to this remarkable work—for two reasons: first, because there are different keys for different minds; and second, because the unexplainable things in many cases come nearer the "mind's eye," as Shakespeare calls it, without words. We cannot tell *why* we understand such and such a thing, but we *do* understand it, and that is enough—quite according to Lewis Carroll's ideas, for he always appeals to our imagination and that is never guided by rules. The higher it soars, the more fantastic the region over which it hovers, the nearer it gets to the land of "make believe," "let's pretend" and "supposing," the better pleased is Lewis Carroll.

In a delightful letter to American children, published in *The Critic* shortly after his death, he gives his own ideas as to the meaning of his writings.

"I'm very much afraid I didn't mean anything but nonsense," he wrote; "still you know words mean more than we mean to express when we use them, so a whole book ought to mean a great deal more than the writer means. So whatever good meanings are in the book, I shall be glad to accept as the meaning of the book. The best that I've seen is by a lady (she published it in a letter to a newspaper) that the whole book is an allegory on the search after happiness."

THE END

julia arenas

alice in wonderland

return to wonderland

www.ingramcontent.com/pod-product-compliance
Lightning Source LLC
Chambersburg PA
CBHW061747020426
42331CB00006B/1379